THE
Archive Photographs
SERIES

WORTHING

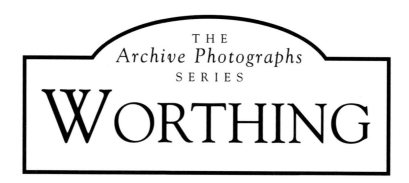

THE
Archive Photographs
SERIES

WORTHING

Compiled by
Chris Hare

CHALFORD

The Chalford Publishing Company
St Mary's Mill, Chalford,
Stroud, Gloucestershire, GL6 8NX

ISBN 0 7524 1043 1

Typesetting and origination by
The Chalford Publishing Company
Printed in Great Britain by
Bailey Print, Dursley, Gloucestershire

Contents

Dedication
To the memory of Terry Child

Introduction

The historian, J.F.C. Harrison, once remarked that some people tended not to read the Introduction to books, which he thought a pity, as the most important part of his book, *The Common People*, was the Introduction. A very important part of this book is the Introduction, because it explains how the unique collection of photographs and sketches it contains came to be published.

Most of the photographs in this volume come from one collection - the Terry Child Collection. Terry was an enthusiastic collector of historical ephemera concerning Worthing and the surrounding district. His collection includes directories, guide books, bills of sale, momentoes of all descriptions and, most importantly, photographs.

When he died in 1993, at the early age of 47, Terry left a collection of 3,000 photographs, most of them in postcard form. Terry had always been extremely generous in allowing authors to borrow his material, never asking anything more in return than a copy of the published work. His collection was so varied and extensive, that there were few aspects of local history for which Terry could not provide an illustration.

After Terry's death, his family and friends were concerned that the collection should not be split up. Fortunately, following conversations with Terry's mother, I was able to put her in touch with Martin Hayes at Worthing Library. The result of those discussions was that the Terry Child Collection, as it became known, came into the ownership of West Sussex County Library Service. Today, the collection, under appropriate supervision, is available to the public.

This is primarily a book of old photographs, spanning the years 1854 to 1987. However, you will notice there are also a number of sketches, most which are the work of A. Elliot. We know very little about the artist and do not even know what his first name was. His sketches are in the ownership of the library service and have been for some time. All the sketches are of Worthing and the surrounding district and date from 1883 to 1920.

I see the sketches as complementary to the photographs, not a substitute. Somehow, when an old view is seen in photographic form next to a sketch of the same scene, we are offered an added dimension - we see a bit more of a lost world. Some of Elliot's work was probably drawn at speed, sketched out on a pad as he walked along the country lanes which used to lead into Worthing. Other pieces, though, are studied compositions, drawn with attention to detail. This is the first time the best of Elliot's Worthing work has been published in one book and, in the case of most of the pieces, the first time they have been published at all.

My role, therefore, is secondary. I provide what are hopefully useful comments and explanations. For younger readers in particular (by which I mean anyone under fifty), the town of today is so different from the one that existed before the Second World War that often no points of reference remain to link an old scene with the present-day view. In some cases whole streets have been demolished; in others, green, open spaces have been transformed into sprawling housing estates. In compiling this book, there were occasions when the enormity of some of the changes caused me to stop and ponder. No other century in the history of England has seen so much change, at such a rapid rate.

I have divided the illustrations into twelve chapters, which I hope makes better use, and therefore better sense, of the material. Wherever possible I have sought to provide original illustrations and not to imitate the excellent pictorial histories produced by Elleray, Blann or Dr White. Imitation may be the highest form of flattery, but it's also a bit cheeky and rather tiresome for the reader, who is left feeling he has, 'seen all this before'. Only where no alternative was available, or where it would simply have been perverse not to use a certain view, have I included a previously published photograph or drawing.

Throughout this book I have tried to provide accurate and informative captions. The illustration on the first page of each chapter is accompanied by a slightly longer caption, which hopefully sets the following views in a proper context.

Chris Hare
October 1997

Acknowledgements

Finally and most importantly, I would like to express my thanks and appreciation to the staff at Worthing Library, for their immense help, patience, and good humour. In particular, I wish to thank Martin Hayes and Robin Knibb, without whose help this book might never have been published.

Photographs published in this book which are not from the Terry Child Collection, or from other collections at Worthing Library, are from the author's own collection. The photographs reproduced on the bottom of page 32 and the bottom of page 43 appear courtesy of Mrs Gina Wilmhurst (née Wingfield), whose family lived in Worthing for many generations. The photograph of the old Tarring fort on page 94, now in Australia, was taken by Mrs Mary Rosenberg of Worthing.

One

Lost Views

An unusual and very early view of about 1800. The artist is standing close to the entrance of Worthing House, which can be seen on the left. In the middle distance can be seen the banks of the Teville stream, while in the far distance can be seen Broadwater church, which in those days had a small spire. Today the Rivoli public house, formerly known as the Lennox stands on the site of Worthing House. The Teville stream now runs in an underground culvert. What was then called North Street, is today the northern part of Chapel Road.

A view of 1824. Note the bathing machines on the beach. The seafront multi-storey car-park and bowling alley built in 1966 would appear as the most prominent building if a view was taken from a similar angle today.

A Regency terrace in Marine Place. These charming seaside dwellings, built of Worthing yellow brick and flint cobbles, were once very common in Worthing. Over the last half century, however, most have been lost to re-development, including the ones shown here in Elliot's sketch of 1920.

Worthing's old Town Hall was demolished in 1966 to make way for the Guildborne Centre development. This photograph was taken in 1854, just prior to the removal of the pump. It is one of the oldest surviving photographs of Worthing.

South Street looking south towards the old kiosks that stood at the entrance of Worthing pier, prior to the construction of the Pavilion in 1926. The buildings on the right were demolished at about the same time and were replaced by the Arcade development.

A rare view of Burden's farmhouse from the east. One of Worthing's original, pre-resort farmhouses, Burden's was demolished in the 1960s. Today, Safeways stands on the site. The Jack Horner public house, on the right of this picture, formerly known as the Anchor, is the only building in this photograph of about 1960 which still stands today.

Richmond House stood on the corner of Richmond Road and Chapel Road and housed the town's library and art gallery. It was demolished to make way for a new, purpose-built building in 1908. When the present library was opened in 1975, the old library was converted into the town's Tourist Information Centre.

The South Street horse trough in about 1930. The trough replaced the pump, which was removed in 1854. About 1906 the electric street light replaced the previous gas light. The trough was replaced by a roundabout just before the Second World War. During the war a reinforced concrete pill-box stood on the roundabout. The well known clock-tower was erected after the war.

The Kursaal Gardens were created when the Kursaal entertainment complex (now the Dome) was built in 1910. The gardens originally fell within the grounds of Bedford House (which can be seen in the background). The gardens were lost in 1922 when the existing roller-skating rink in the Dome was enlarged and modified to create the present-day cinema auditorium.

The Navarino Windmills in East Worthing, shortly before their demolition at the turn of the century. Ham Road is on the right. Worthing once had many windmills, most of which were still standing a century ago. Motor-driven mills and cheap grain and flour imports combined to bring about the rapid decline in windmilling. By 1915 only the High Salvington Mill remained.

Worthing Hospital, Lyndhurst Road in 1914. The name 'Hospital' was introduced in 1904; prior to that the name 'Worthing Infirmary and Dispensary' was the official title. The building was due for demolition in 1997.

The sea end of South Street in about 1935. The Marine Hotel on the right was one of Worthing's two original hotels (the other, the Royal Sea House, was destroyed by fire in 1901). This imposing Regency building was replaced by an inferior successor in 1965, which was itself demolished in the early 1980s.

The old lifeboat and coastguard station, at the bottom of Heene Road (then Heene Lane). The absence of Heene Terrace to the left of the picture dates this photograph to before 1865.

Heene Lane in about 1870, or possibly earlier. The buildings on the right of the picture still stand and have been converted into shops and a public house. The villa on the left also survives and is situated on the corner of Bath Road and Heene Road.

An undated Elliot sketch, simply entitled 'Lane to sea from Heene'. If this is one of his earlier works from the 1880s, this scene could be the northern end of what is now Heene Road. By the early 1900s development along the entire length of the Heene Road was all but complete.

Heene Road in transition. The contrast between the thatched cottage on the right and the late Victorian suburbs on the left could not be more apparent. Compare also the traditional (and crumbling) flint stone wall on the right with the more decorative flint and brick wall on the left.

Isted's or Heene Mill, shortly before its demolition in 1903. A mill had stood on this spot since Tudor times. 'Windmill House' today stands on the site in Mill Road.

In this high quality photograph of Heene mill, new housing can be seen enroaching on the mill's rural setting.

A view from Elm Grove in about 1920, looking south towards Wallace Avenue, with Mill Road to the left and Goring Lane (now Road) to the right. None of the buildings or trees in this picture exist today.

Two
The Pier

STEAMER APPROACHING PIER, WORTHING

Worthing's first pier was opened in 1862. It was a very modest affair (see the 'weatherspout' picture in Chapter Five). In 1889 the pier was both lengthened and widened, with the addition of a sea-end pavilion, and two rather attractive kiosks at its entrance. Little of this pier survives today, having either been wrecked by storms or destroyed by fire. Pleasure trips by paddle steamer were very popular with the Victorians. The extension of the pier in 1889 allowed these vessels to 'dock' at Worthing, thereby enhancing the town's reputation as a seaside resort.

The Worthing Pier Master in 1883

Elliot's sketch of the Worthing pier master in 1883. Although a simple drawing it seems to convey a great deal about the old man whose responsibility it was to collect entrance fees to the pier. He is clean shaven, except for two large sideburns that meet under the chin. This type of beard was once common among working men locally, although its popularity was declining by the 1880s.

The 1889 pier on a summer's day. Notice the paddle steamer about to dock. The right-hand kiosk to the forefront of the picture sold admission tickets, while its neighbour sold newspapers and tobacco. The pier was owned by a limited company, whose directors tended to be councillors or council officials.

The wrecked pier. A great storm on the night of 22/23 March 1913 brought down the central girders, leaving the pavilion at the sea-end marooned.

The full extent of the destruction was only apparent at low tide the following morning. A freak wave, as well as the storm itself, was blamed for an event, which, if it had happened during the day, could have led to a terrible loss of life.

Worthing Pier Wrecked, March 22, 1913

The previous night, Worthing people had heard the awesome sound of the pier collapsing; now, they gathered in hushed groups to survey the extent of the destruction. At a time when town pride was felt far more keenly than today, the general mood was one of determination that a replacement pier should be speedily erected.

The surviving portion of the pier was surrounded by the sea at high tide and, with Easter approaching, the people soon dubbed it 'Easter Island'. This photograph was taken from the air by the Pashley brothers in their aeroplane. It is one of the town's earliest aerial photographs.

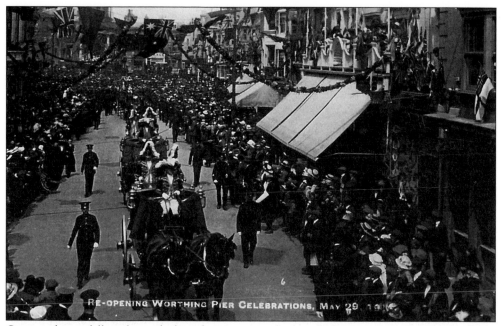

RE-OPENING WORTHING PIER CELEBRATIONS, MAY 29 1914

Civic pride was fully redeemed when the pier was re-built in little over a year. On 29 May 1914, the Lord Mayor of London opened the new pier with full ceremonial splendour. It was a day of great rejoicing.

"LEAVING WARNES HOTEL"

OPENING OF NEW PIER WORTHING BY THE LORD MAYOR OF LONDON · MAY·29·1914·

This picture shows the Lord Mayor's coach leaving the Warne's Hotel. Notice that the policemen are wearing caps rather than helmets. From 1913 until the mid-1930s, caps were the standard issue. Helmets were re-introduced following the street brawling associated with the Fascist movement after 1933.

Hats were universal in 1914. From the plumed hats of the Lord Mayor's footman, to the flat caps of the working men; only the poorest of men were seen bare-headed.

In 1933 disaster struck again. Ironically it was the very part of the pier, the sea-end pavilion, which had escaped the ravages of 1913, which was destroyed by a fire.

Pictures of Worthing's blazing pier made front-page news in the national newspapers. Other piers had suffered fires in the long hot summer of 1933, but none as destructive as Worthing's. The wind fanned the flames and there were claims that there had been a twenty minute delay in calling out the fire brigade.

Volunteers were drafted in to rip up the wooden planks in the deck of the pier, in order to stop the fire spreading. *The Worthing Herald* reported that 'They included visitors in holiday dress, a bus conductor in uniform, one or two men in bathing costume, and one stripped except for his trousers.'

PIER FIRE, WORTHING. SEPT. 10TH 33. 7.

On arrival at the scene, the Fire Brigade soon realised all was lost, as *The Worthing Herald* related: '"We haven't got a chance!", exclaimed a fireman, and as if to prove the truth of his words, the whole front of the Pavilion flashed into flames, and a minute later the entire building was enveloped.'

WORTHING PIER, DESTROYED BY FIRE. SEPT. 10TH. 1933.

The heat of the fire was so intense that the pavilion was almost entirely consumed. A new pavilion was later erected in an art deco style and survives to the present day.

The southern pavilion was opened in 1926 and was built to resemble its northern equivalent. The style of the new southern pavilion was very different, so the symmetry of the two pavilions only lasted for seven years. Note the white-topped 'tram-o-car' in the forefront of the picture. These little buses ran along Marine Parade in the inter-war years.

The pier has frequently formed the backdrop to many a seaside photograph. In this picture, taken near Splash Point about ninety years ago, the unusual head-gear of the ladies on the left is of interest.

Another shot, again close to Splash Point, and at about the same time. It seems odd to the modern mind that people should sit on the beach in hot sunshine, wearing so many clothes! The boys in their blazers, shirts and ties, look especially out of place to us today.

Worthing Town Council imposed strict by-laws concerning the decency of bathers. The sign on the right indicating 'Ladies Only', is a reminder that the sexes were strictly separated on the beach. Young children were the only exception. Bexhill's decision to allow mixed bathing in 1898 caused uproar in Worthing.

Three
Royalty and Mayoralty

We can safely say that Royalist sentiment and civic pride were a good deal more manifest at the start of the twentieth century than at its close. The celebration of the Coronation of George V in June 1911 was marked by much pomp and ceremony in Worthing, as this picture of the Worthing constabulary marching out demonstrates. The later Royal visits of the inter-war years caused great excitement and a sense of honour amongst the townspeople. The Town Council never enjoyed that degree of loyalty, but respect for councillors and aldermen was far higher than it is today, probably because the powers and responsibilities of the Council were far more wide-reaching than they are at present.

This photograph showing children holding Union flags and other national insignia probably dates either to Queen Victoria's Diamond Jubilee of 1897, or King Edward VII's coronation of 1902. Note the school governess on the right and the rather perplexed little girl on the left.

This writer assumed that Worthing's 'Ivy Arch', which later gave its name to the urban road built around it, had been erected to commemorate Queen Victoria's Golden Jubilee of 1887. Further research indicates that it was built some twenty years or more earlier, by Dr Cyrus Elliott, who purchased the land known as The Quashetts (a name that still survives in the present-day footpath that runs from Broadwater Street East to Little High Street), and built the Arch as a piece of Victorian eccentricity. The Arch was only demolished as recently as 1967.

Sir Aubrey Fletcher being received at Worthing Town Hall in January 1906, following his success in being elected as Member of Parliament for the Lewes division, which at that time included Worthing. It is something of a paradox that the general interest in elections and campaign meetings was greater at a time when most people did not have the vote, than today when all adults enjoy the franchise.

A rare, possibly unique picture of the visit to Worthing by King Edward VII in December 1908. Presumably His Majesty is inside the car amidst the crowd of people.

Only eighteen months after his visit, the King was dead. Worthing displayed its grief with lavish displays of solemn pomp. Here we see the procession of mourning passing up Chapel Road. The old Town Hall is on the left.

The funeral of Sergeant Frederick Hews, 9 September 1911. This was the last processional funeral in Worthing, attended by the Duke of Norfolk's own band. Hews, a member of the Sussex Volunteers (a forerunner of the present-day territorials), was a personal friend of the Duke. His death at the early age of twenty nine was keenly felt by his friends and family. The cortège is seen heading south, down Clifton Road.

The Great War only officially came to an end with the signing of the Peace of Versailles on 19 July 1919, although the actual fighting had ceased with the Armistice of 11 November the previous year. Great crowds gathered to hear the Mayor read out the conditions of the Peace. In the photograph it is possible to see the Mayor raising his hand, presumably in an effort to make himself heard over the enthusiastic cheering of the crowd.

Mrs Ellen Chapman became Worthing's first female councillor in 1910 and its first female Mayor in 1920. A formidable proponent of female suffrage, she was ridiculed when she attempted to become Mayor in 1914, but acclaimed six years later; indeed she was re-elected for a further term. The invaluable effort of women during the Great War had softened the opposition not just to women voting, but even to a woman becoming Mayor of Worthing. She is pictured with the Mayor of Rienebourg l'Avoue.

The Duke and Duchess of York visited Worthing in May 1928. The future King and Queen (and present Queen Mother) visited the Prince Albert Convalescent Home, a charity actively supported by the Duke. The Duke and Duchess were also formally welcomed to Worthing outside the Pavilion by Alderman Frost, the Mayor. The Dome cinema can be seen to the left, in the background of this picture.

The creation of Greater Worthing, as it was called in 1929, trebled the size of the borough. The parish councils of Goring and Durrington were abolished and a new Worthing Town Council, which included those places, was elected. The councillors are sitting in the council chamber of the old Town Hall.

34

Earl Winterton, MP for Worthing and Horsham, opening Worthing's new Town Hall in 1933. At the time the £120,000 spent on the building was highly controversial. As well as the cost of the building, others objected to its appearance, one critic describing it as looking like a barracks. It is now a grade II listed building.

Another visit by the Duchess of York, this time to Gifford House in April 1934. She is seen being welcomed by Alderman Duffield and his wife, the Mayor and Mayoress.

The Duchess chats informally with staff and volunteers at Gifford House. Such an engaging style was in marked contrast to the stern aloofness Royalty had adopted in the past.

Celebrations for George V's Silver Jubilee in 1935. Crowds gather outside the Pavilion, many dressed in uniform or in historical costume.

Crowds line Marine Parade to watch the Jubilee procession and floats pass by.

The Jubilee procession passes down Chapel Road. The second float, entitled 'The Silver Screen - The Silver Jubilee' probably caught the spirit of the times more accurately than 'Clive of India'.

A Sussex trug maker demonstrates his skills to the Mayor, Alderman W.G. Tree, in 1937. The Town Clerk, Mr J. Kennedy Allerton, looks on. In the background can be seen the Deputy Mayor, Councillor Bennett, and, wearing a ceremonial top hat, the mace-bearer.

Ten Sussex Mayors, including those of Worthing, gather at County Hall prior to a service of dedication for the Festival of Britain celebrations in the county. Despite the livery, robes, chains of office and official mace bearers, most of the Sussex mayoralties were not even a hundred years old when this photograph was taken in 1951.

Four

It Made the News

This German aeroplane, brought down near the Golf Links at the time of the Battle of Britain, in fact, hardly made the news, as one might have expected. Firstly, there were many similar incidents taking place across the county and, secondly, much of the news was censored, with only the vaguest of descriptions being given as to the time and place of such events. Conversely, events that most of us would consider rather minor or even trivial today, once caused great interest and controversy. In the days before the mass media, most people had only a hazy idea of events in other parts of the country.

Attempts by a Lancing farmer to close a footpath over his land caused a great deal of ill-feeling in Worthing during the 1880s. The sea had washed away much of the coast road, so for many people the Lancing path was the most direct link with Shoreham and beyond. Fences put up by the landowner were routinely broken down by protesters. On one occasion the farmer was even burnt in effigy by an angry crowd. The matter took years to resolve through the courts, but eventually the protesters won the day.

Colonnade House, on the corner of Warwick Street and High Street, after it was gutted by fire in January 1888. Although repaired and rebuilt, The Colonnade never again recaptured its old splendour. It was one of the first imposing houses to be built in Worthing, along with Warwick House, which stood opposite.

The Royal Sea House Hotel, along with The Marine, was one of Worthing's first high-class hotels. It was gutted by fire in 1901. Hundreds came to watch the forlorn attempts of the fire brigade to save the hotel. For over twenty years the site stood derelict, until the building of the present-day Arcade.

The great fire at Goring Hall, caught by Elliot's pen in August 1885 caused a sensation at the time. People ran from a service at Goring church to help fight the blaze. The fire engines from both Littlehampton and Worthing were summoned. They linked their hoses together in order to pump water from a pond about half a mile distant. Despite this valiant effort the Hall was gutted.

Worthing Town Council in 1890. These distinguished-looking gentleman were not universally admired. A certain section of Worthing society referred to them as the 'Forty Thieves', a derogatory term that is still known to some of the town's older citizens. The origin of this jibe seems to have arisen during the events surrounding the terrible typhoid epidemic of 1893, which claimed hundreds of victims during the summer of that year.

'The Fever', as it was known, was caused by the contamination of some of the town's wells. There had been voices calling for a proper reservoir and pumping station to be built on the Downs, north of Worthing. But this would cost money and would mean a hefty hike in the Rates, something some councillors, even after the epidemic, resisted. Eventually, however, a public outcry forced them to act and the first borehole was sunk on the Downs.

This biting satirical cartoon of 1895 accuses senior councillors and the Town Clerk, William Verrall, of profiting in the wake of the typhoid epidemic. It was claimed that certain properties belonging to victims of the Fever were later 'acquired' by the 'Forty Thieves', who gained a good income from rents received and later the sale of land and properties. Even the way the Relief Fund was handled was questioned. The councillor in the centre of the picture is seen handing Alderman Patching (four times Mayor of Worthing) a cheque, while Patching in turn is handing a widow a token for some free coal. Meanwhile a skeleton, representing death, is seen gesturing from the open doorway.

Feelings in Worthing were running very high. One councillor's home was besieged by an angry mob. In response to public pressure, work was begun in 1896 to build a pumping station and reservoir, on the downs north of Broadwater. The station was officially opened by the Duke of Cambridge on 26 April 1897. Henceforth Worthing people would enjoy pure unpolluted drinking water, straight from the Downs. This photograph shows the construction of the water works during the summer of 1896.

Motor traffic accidents became more frequent as the number of motor vehicles on the roads increased. Given the speed of motor vehicles compared to horse-drawn ones, and the lack of basic training, this was hardly surprising. Char-a-bancs, such as this one, pictured in Heene Road in 1909 seem to have been particularly accident prone.

Worthing gained its first lifeboat in 1850, following the *Lalla Rookh* disaster, in which eleven Worthing fishermen lost their lives attempting to save the crew of this stricken vessel. For the next eighty years, Worthing people would always flock to the shoreline whenever the lifeboat was launched.

Return of Worthing Lifeboat after "Rescue". July 23rd 1920.

Most lifeboat launches were successful and without casualty, but danger always attended any launch in rough weather. The first lifeboat house was at Heene (see page 15), but a purpose-built one was later erected closer to the pier and can still be recognised today by its curious observation turret, although it is now a private residence.

Worthing Lifeboat—Off to the Wreck, Aug. 6, 1912.

This launch of the lifeboat in strong winds and an incoming tide in August 1912 was only made possible by the crowds on the pier, who attached ropes to the lifeboat and heaved it into deeper water.

In February 1915, the lifeboat capsized attempting to rescue the *Kingsmill*, which was later beached on the sands at Goring. *The Worthing Gazette* reported the dreadful moment: 'Then a big sea caught them and took the boat over, throwing them into the water. The sails and mast were immersed, but the boat, being of the self-righting type, was soon upright again'. Yet one of the crew, Jack Burgess, was lost, and drowned in the icy sea.

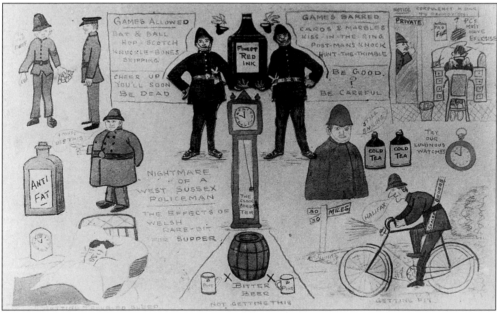

Yet more scandal, this time concerning the police. In 1913, a new Chief Constable, W.S. Williams, was appointed in West Sussex. He immediately set to task to root out ill-discipline and laxness amongst his men. A superintendent at Worthing was reduced to the rank of Sergeant for allowing his men to play cards and drink beer at the police station. An Inspector was demoted for drinking in a public bar. Henceforth, declared Williams, all constables must follow a strict conduct code, to include being in bed by 10 pm every night, unless of course they were on duty!

If car accidents were a novelty before the First World War, just imagine the excitement caused by a plane crash. The Pashley brothers frequently flew from Shoreham, to places as far away as Salisbury. This plane came down on 22 July 1914, less than a fortnight before the outbreak of the Great War.

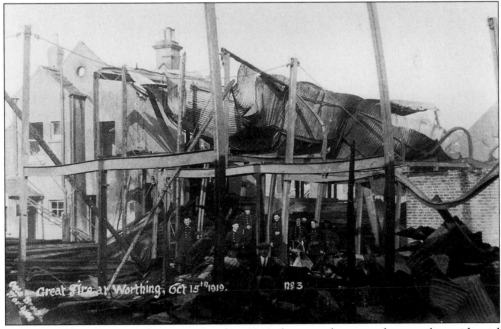

A fire at a Worthing warehouse in October 1919 threatened to spread to nearby residential properties in Southcourt Road. Fortunately, the fire brigade had just taken possession of a new engine which was much better equipped to deal with large fires than its predecessor.

Great Fire at Worthing, Oct 15th 1919.
/n81

A view of the fire from Southcourt Road. The top storey of the house on the right was later demolished, but the bottom floor was converted into a bungalow and survives to the present day.

Everyone loves the circus, especially when the elephants join you on the beach! The arrival of the circus was always big news. Photographs of elephants processing through Worthing were often to be found in local newspapers earlier in this century.

Five
Wild Weather

This chapter could almost be called 'Storms', for many of the following pictures were taken following the great storms of 1913, 1931 and 1987. This picture is from 1987 and was taken in Ilex Way, where so many of the great Ilex oaks were felled on the night of 16 October.

Waterspouts are rare, especially in the English Channel. This one seen off Worthing in 1864 was captured by an artist from the *Illustrated Times*. A waterspout can best be described as a seaborne tornado.

The weather really does seem to have been colder in the first half than the second half of the twentieth century. The freezing of the sea in January 1907 was, however, unusual, even for the times.

Another picture from the same series. Possibly the cross marks the lodgings of the man in the photograph.

People enjoying the snow on the Downs north of Worthing in 1916.

A woman and her baby seem in some danger as an angry sea threatens to engulf them on 'Faggot Walk' in 1905. In an effort to protect the path from the ravages of the sea, piles of faggots were driven into the shingle - hence the name. The path ran from Splash Point to the Half Brick. Years later loosened faggots were still being washed ashore at Worthing.

A Gale in March 1913 is best remembered for its destruction of Worthing Pier (see Chapter Two). It also caused damage along the seafront, to shelters and the bandstand. At nearby Lancing, makeshift bungalows made out of old railway carriages were tossed into the sea.

During a storm on 10 November 1931, the sea broke through, sweeping away Faggot Walk and flooding the Brighton Road from the Half Brick to Splash Point.

Buses had to navigate water several inches deep. Flooding has been a persistent threat to Worthing for years: during the 1990s, hundreds of thousands of pounds have been spent in strengthening sea defences.

The 1931 Storm brought down a fair number of trees, including these near Sompting.

Another photograph at Sompting. If anyone can identity the house in the background, the author would be pleased to hear from them.

At the time of writing, the Great Storm of 1987 happened only ten years ago. Yet, to First and Middle School children it is already history - as most of them were not even born in 1987. This photograph was taken opposite the Pier Pavilion, where the force of the wind had snapped a reinforced concrete lamp post.

Dislodged masonry litters the street in Western Place.

Beach huts were reduced to matchwood and remains of huts and even fishing boats were found some several hundred metres inland.

This row of trees on Broadwater Green fell like skittles under the force of the wind.

Residents emerged shell-shocked from their homes, to view the devastation in Sea Lane. Several mighty trees lay across the road.

More Goring residents come to terms with the night's destruction.

Goring churchyard was a mass of twisted branches and crushed gravestones. This man certainly appears to have a task on his hands to shift it all!

One of the great Ilex Way trees, planted in about 1840, dwarfs the figure standing on its upturned roots.

Six
Recreation

'People used to make their own entertainment' is a cliché which happens to be true. Before the arrival of cinema and radio, or even popular daily newspapers, ordinary people had to make their own entertainment. Some of this was communal and local, taking the guise of carnivals, fairs and festivals. The emergence of the Football Association in the 1880s was the start of a more nationally centred form of recreation. This photograph of a fair, possibly at Broadwater, dates from about 1900.

Look closely at this picture. Emerging from the darkness you will see a wild band of revellers, dressed in fantastic garb, carrying banners and flags. Behind them you will discern an effigy on a pole, followed by a great moving mass of fire, illuminating the darkness. This is Bonfire Night in Worthing, drawn by Elliot in 1883. Some years later, following the notorious 'Skeleton Army' riots, the old wild and anarchic bonfire celebrations were suppressed, yet a hint of those wanton days is recalled in this picture.

The spirit of disguise and mummery did not die with Bonfire Night, but lingered on another twenty or thirty years in the annual carnivals held by the Friendly and Mutual Societies. The blackening of faces is a very ancient and simple form of disguise, once pregnant with menacing overtones. Such associations had faded by the time this photograph was taken about ninety years ago.

60

A far more modest and 'decent' carnival day in 1919. The Great War did much to break old traditions, not just because war itself usually hastens change, but also because so many of the young men who would normally have participated in the observance of old customs had been killed in the fighting.

If street festivals suited the tastes of the common people, the middle class preferred dramatic performance and recitals. The performer, dressed either as a soldier, or possibly as a postman, is, as Elliot informs us in a note on the back of his sketch, singing a comic song. That being the case, the audience do not look too amused, while the panel of gentlemen on the right (are they fellow performers, or maybe judges?), look sceptical to say the least. Elliot however, tells us that, 'the concert was a decided success'.

36. Splash Point, Worthing.

For the Victorians and Edwardians the Promenade was the place to be. It was the place where people met friends, or displayed their latest fashions - a place to see and be seen. In this photograph a sedate group at Splash Point observe the comings and goings along Faggot Walk.

The Promenade on a summer's day. Notice the dark, heavy clothing of the people in this picture. Even the boy on the left is wearing a shirt and tie, blazer and cap. The building on the right is the Marlborough House - a superior 'Boarding Establishment'.

62

A close-up of the Marlborough House and the Bandstand. Worthing's ornate bandstand was a major attraction in the town, attracting residents and visitors alike. The Lido was later built on the site. A multi-storey car-park and bowling alley now stand opposite.

WORTHING. THE PARK LAKE.

Worthing's People's Park, later renamed Homefield Park was a very beautiful place of recreation, with an ornamental lake and carefully maintained borders and shrubs. Much of the park was lost when the hospital was extended.

Shooting was a very popular sport. Just as their ancestors had practised with longbows on the village green, so the Victorians set up rifle ranges. From an early age, boys were encouraged to take up rifle shooting. This photograph of 1867 shows the Sussex team at the annual championships at Wimbledon.

A photograph of 1908 includes, on the right, Alderman Alfred Cortis, Worthing's first Mayor, a keen marksman, who once won the silver medal at Wimbledon and first competed in 1861.

Football was once a game with few rules and dozens, even hundreds, of participants. The emergence of the Football Association saw football established as a spectator sport. The twentieth century has seen spectator sports become the norm - an idea very alien to our ancestors.

Worthing's 3-2 victory over Helmston in April 1907 is captured in this photograph. The men on the right with baskets were presumably selling refreshments to the crowd.

Athletics also became increasingly popular from the late nineteenth century onwards. This group of runners are pictured outside the Cricketers at Broadwater.

Worthing's first 'Motor-Carnival' was held in 1905. Perhaps nothing symbolises the twentieth century more than the motor car. These carnivals were organised by the Warnes Hotel. Huge crowds came to marvel at the new machines, gaily decked out in flowers and streamers.

This shot, taken at the carnival on a wet day in September 1908, shows an interesting view of Warwick Street. In the far distance can be seen the trees that once graced the centre of the Broadway. Half way down, on the left, can be seen the sign of the Warwick (now the Hogshead Emporium). Next to that are the three characteristic golden balls of a pawnbrokers shop.

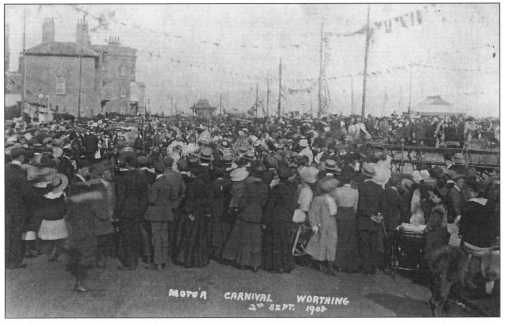

An unidentified event of 1921. A note on the back, written by Terry Child, tells us that the man in the middle is 'Jimmie Joyce', who was almost certainly a sportsman of some kind. The author would be pleased to hear from anyone who knows his identity.

Hawaiin Night at the Ritz Dance Hall in 1948. All very tame by modern standards, but the advent of the night-club offered a new form of recreation, aimed at younger people.

Seven
Trades

In the days before big department stores and national and international corporations, most people worked for a local employer, or worked for themselves. The Worthing fishing fleet once kept several families in full-time employment. Curiously, nearly all these families had surnames beginning with the letter 'B', such as Belton, Bashford, Burgess, Blann, and Benn. The fishermen from the different Sussex fishing towns all had their own nick-names. The Worthing fisherman were called 'pork-bolters', due to their superstitious fear of seeing a pig before they set sail.

Mr Vine, a caterer, and Mrs Waverley, who kept a tea room, combined their talents to open a Temperance Hotel at 10 Chapel Road. Temperance was a very strong political and social movement in England at one time, but its influence sharply declined after the Great War. The Temperance Hotel had closed by 1935.

Dorsett's butchers shop at the turn of the century. Notice the pig's head hanging up over the door on the left - yours for only tuppence!

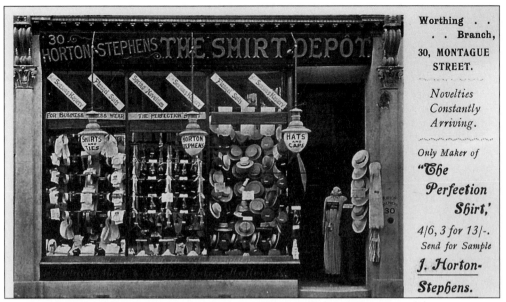

Horton-Stephens' 'Shirt Depot' at 30 Montague Street. The notices in the window inform us that the maker of 'The Perfection Shirt' is also offering suits, hosiery and 'spring novelties'.

Bicycles became increasingly popular from the 1890s onwards. Here we see Mr Springford outside his shop on the corner of Milton Road and Brunswick Place.

Mr Milner, harness and boot maker, outside his shop at 33 West Buildings in about 1920.

Miss G.H. Austin, outside her hairdressing shop at 77 Montague Street in about 1905.

Glaudia Symonds outside Knowles' baker's shop at 217 Tarring Road in 1924. Knowles remained in business until the 1970s.

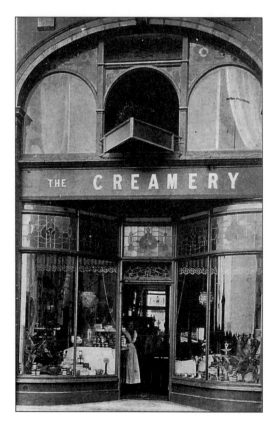

The Creamery at 10 Chapel Road, which was a quality tea room, offering home-made preserves.

Although not immediately apparent in black and white, this picture shows a crop of Worthing cucumbers. Market Gardening was once a major employer in Worthing from the 1870s onwards. Worthing tomatoes and cucumbers were famous and much sought after across the country.

Carl Adolf Seebold, perhaps Worthing's most successful businessman this century. This Swiss-German began by organising concert parties on the pier and later became the owner of Worthing's 'palace' cinemas, of which the Rivoli at the northern end of Chapel Road was the most sumptuous.

A group of Worthing busmen in the 1920s.
The man on the right bears an uncanny
resemblance to the Liberal-Unionist
politician, Joseph Chamberlain.

Oilman, Thomas Huggett operated from 72 Station Road. The increasing popularity of
electricity for heating, lighting and even cooking, must have undermined Huggett's trade and
he had ceased trading by 1935.

A milkman in the days before electric floats. Several dairies operated in the Worthing area and, despite the quaintness of this picture, rivalry between the dairies was often intense.

13 North Street, from where Joan Strange worked as an osteopath. The building still survives today, but is hardly recognisable. It is presently in use as the offices of Worthing's Citizen's Advice Bureau. During the war, Miss Strange kept a detailed diary of everyday events, extracts of which were published in book form in 1989, under the title, *Dispatches from the Home Front*.

The Celebrated Broadwater Sweet Shop Near Worthing.

Older residents will remember with affection Luff's homemade sweets, sold at their Broadwater shop. Also remembered will be the Whitehouse sweet factory in Church Road, Tarring, which closed as recently as 1969.

Religion played a far more dominant role in daily life than it does today. These three men were members of the Church Army, an organisation established by the Anglican Church in response to the growing popularity of the Salvation Army.

The staff of the Prince Albert Convalescent Home in about 1905. Throughout this century, Worthing has been known as a town with a large elderly and infirm population. The role of the policeman in this picture is unclear, but he looks as if he is 'feeling the collar' of the gentleman to his right.

The Stanhoe Hotel and Motor Garage. The hotel trade can be traced back, not surprisingly, to Worthing's earliest days as a seaside resort. It was also common in the early years of motoring for hotels to offer a 'motor garage' service, often because hotels were some of the first establishments to own motor cars.

Eight
Broadwater and Offington

48. Broadwater Cross, Worthing.

For centuries, Worthing was a small coastal hamlet lying within the parish of Broadwater. Even after Worthing officially became a town in 1803, Broadwater's dominance was only slowly eroded. The incorporation of Worthing in 1890 excluded Broadwater and it was not until 1902 that Broadwater was brought under the civil and parochial jurisdiction of Worthing. This photograph, taken at about that time, shows the great trees that used to surround Broadwater churchyard and the triangular hedge that separated Broadwater Road from Broadwater Street. We can imagine that the two ladies hurrying into view, holding their coats over their arms, may have walked the mile from Worthing railway station and were perhaps visiting friends in Broadwater.

Broadwater Street Post Office in about 1900. In those days the mail was collected from the boxes on an almost hourly basis, starting at about 6 am and ending at 10 pm. Local letters, unless posted very late, were expected to arrive the same day.

Broadwater cricket team in 1877. Broadwater's Green was reputed to be the largest in England and therefore of sufficient size to accommodate a full cricket match. Famously, in 1837, Sussex took on the rest of the country at Broadwater, and won.

80

47. *Broadwater Green, Worthing.*

Cricket again on the Green, this time in the 1920s. The Green itself was purchased from the then Lord of the Manor of Broadwater by public subscription in 1864. This effort resulted from local indignation at the neglected state of the Green and also from a fear that the expansion of Worthing might one day make the Green a very attractive site for developers.

Despite the protection afforded to Broadwater Green in 1864, parts of it have been lost to development, chiefly road widening. The duelling of this stretch of Broadwater Street West was at the expense of the Green and also of the drinking fountain, seen on the left, which was removed at the same time.

Offington Corner, Broadwater, with the western end of Broadwater Green on the left. In the distance can be seen the Lodge House of Offington Hall. Just past the Lodge stood the 'Midsummer Tree', around which skeletal apparitions were said to dance on Mid-Summer's Eve.

OFFINGTON CORNER, WORTHING.

This photograph must be slightly later than the previous view, for not only can we now see a telegraph pole by the Lodge, but a letter box has been added to the lamp-post.

A view by the Lodge, looking down Offington Drive. Since the 1930s, the entire estate has been developed. Offington Drive is now a residential road of up-market properties.

A view across Offington Park to Offington Hall. The Gaisford family were the last residents of the Hall and the last Lords of the Manor of Offington. The piecemeal development of the estate, culminating in the demolition of the Hall itself just over thirty years ago, can be reflected upon with regret.

It is hard to believe that this idyllic scene, in the heart of Offington Park, is now a mass of suburban development.

The southern boundary of Offington Park, at Shady Lane. This tree-lined lane ran from Broadwater Green to the cross roads with Tarring Street (now Rectory Road) and Offington Lane. As the lane continued westwards it became Littlehampton Road. Until the Thomas a Becket public house was built in 1911, this cross-roads was as rural as any in the county.

This sketch of Shady Lane by Elliot was drawn in the summer. On a hot day, many a pedestrian must have been pleased by the shade offered in this peaceful lane. Not so today, as traffic streams down the re-named 'Poulters Lane' and the trees are hopelessly outnumbered by the houses.

OFFINGTON CORNER, WORTHING.

Offington Corner, Salvington. The western Lodge, looking westwards along the Arundel Road. Offington Lane is to the left and the Findon Road to the right.

A modern day group of cyclists' would not be advised to re-create this pose - as gaps in the A27 traffic are few and far between!

A final view, this time from the north. Notice that when this photograph was taken, what is now the A27 was an unmade road.

The Golf Links on the Downs north of Broadwater. Worthing Golf Club was established at the turn of the century, while the council-run Hill Barn course opened in 1935. Notice the old Broadwater Mill to the left of the picture.

Broadwater Mill in a sorry state of decay, just prior to its demolition in 1914. The twenty preceding years saw the loss of all of Worthing's old mills, with the exception of High Salvington Mill.

Another 1914 view of the doomed Broadwater Mill.

Broadwater Road before the First World War. This view, looking northwards, is still largely rural in character, although the ornate railings and walls to the left indicate the beginning of residential development, which would eventually merge Worthing and Broadwater into one town.

Nine

Tarring

Parsonage Row, Tarring, in 1895. This photograph can be precisely dated to the demolition of the southern end of the Row in that year. You can see that the furthest gable was in the process of being dismantled when this photograph was taken. The construction of Glebe Road was the reason for the demolition, which included the butcher's shop, a premises unchanged since it was first built in the reign of Henry VI. Tarring however is extremely fortunate in that so many of its ancient buildings still survive. None of the other villages which have been swallowed up by Worthing during the course of the twentieth century have fared as well.

Elliot sketched this view in 1897. Notice the inn sign of the George and Dragon on the right of the picture. Following tradition, the sign is suspended over the street. Today, however, the sign is fixed into an upright position. During the 1920s, when motor traffic was increasing, double-decker buses had to mount the pavement to pass each other in the street, with the result that the inn sign was forever being hit. A frustrated landlord in about 1927 welded it into the upright position we see today.

In order to relieve the congestion in the High Street, the Town Council proposed demolishing all the buildings, including Parsonage Row on the east side of the street, thereby allowing the road to be widened. Opposition to these plans, led by the Sussex Archaeological Society, which had recently purchased the Row, caused a change of heart and the decision to build the present-day Rectory Road as a by-pass for the village. Sadly, the construction of the new road entailed the demolition of a few old buildings, including this cottage.

Elliot's sketch of Bishop's Garth in South Street in 1920. Behind the old cottage were the famous Fig Gardens, which date to 1745 and probably to much earlier. Legend insists that they were originally planted by St Thomas a Becket, although this seems very unlikely.

Judging by the lady's dress, this photograph of Bishop's Garth was probably taken some years before Elliot's sketch. The Gardens, run for many years by Mr and Mrs Wadey, were a very popular tourist attraction. Edward Lear stayed here for several months, sketching the fig trees and visiting his mistress in Brighton.

Inside the Fig Gardens. The notice claims that the tree in the forefront was planted by Becket in 1162. Despite this precise date, there is no evidence for the claim. A more likely originator of the Fig Gardens is St Richard, Bishop of Chichester, who, having fallen out with Henry III, sought refuge at the Bishop's Palace at Tarring. Today only a remnant of the Fig Gardens remain, as the majority of trees were felled in 1988 to make way for modern mews-style development.

The High Street, looking south in 1897. The timber-framed building on the right was known as Stents Cottages and was demolished in 1925. Its neighbour, a thatched barn, went in about 1900 and was replaced by Victoria Terrace.

Stents Cottages again, this time looking northwards. Whereas the southern end of High Street has been remarkably well preserved over the last sixty years, the northern end has been largely rebuilt, although, it has to be said, with modern buildings of an appropriate design.

An early photograph of St Andrew's taken from Church Road. In this photograph, a fence, rather than a flint wall, surrounds the churchyard and the large trees that today grace the spot have yet to be planted. On the right in the foreground there appears to be a large compost heap or dung hill.

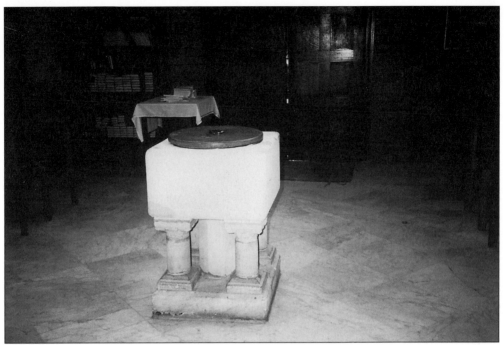

The original Tarring font. The font found in the church today is Victorian; the original was taken to Australia by the Henty family. The Hentys lived at Church House and were Lords of the Manor. When they emigrated to Australia in 1829/31, they took with them just about everything they could, including flocks of sheep, small trees, and the font. The font is now in Trinity College Chapel, Melbourne University.

The Bowling Green to the south of the church. This lovely spot for recreation has been marred in recent years by vandalism and the taunting of the bowlers by groups of juveniles.

Tarring Recreation Ground when it was still a field. Cattle can just be observed in the distance.

A group photograph outside the Bishop's Palace, possibly as early as the 1850s. The Palace dates from 1230, which makes it early, but not as early as Thomas a Becket, who was murdered at Canterbury sixty years earlier. The Palace was in use as a school from 1779 until 1985. One wonders if the discovery in 1963 of a pit of old champagne bottles had anything to do with the ladies and gentlemen in this picture!

This Elliot sketch is at first baffling, for the artist simply described it as being near Tarring. The cottage in the distance however solved the mystery. It still stands on the Littlehampton Road (no. 101), just to the west of the junction with Lindum Road. Drawn in 1920, the scene would be unrecognisable today were it not for the survival of that lone dwelling.

Another Elliot drawing, this time of the Littlehampton Road itself. The work is not dated, but is probably of about 1900 or earlier. Whatever the year, it is a remarkable image of what is today such a busy and congested road.

Tarring, Salvington and Durrington Hospital Day Parade, 7 September 1912. The local Army volunteers and the Sons of Temperance, Sussex Division, can be seen in the parade. Before the days of the Welare State, raising money for the Hospital was simply a matter of enlightened self-interest. The recently built Thomas a Becket Hotel can be seen - a hint of the urbanisation to come.

Following the near humiliation of the British Army during the Boer War and the growing military might of Germany, greater emphasis began to be attached to the Volunteer Reserve Corps (the VRC). During the summer months large scale exercises would be held, bringing men from all over the country. In 1907 the VRC came to Tarring. These men are obviously the catering contingent.

Officers and cadets prepare to 'move out'. The location is not stated, but it may be by Chippers farmhouse.

The church helps to pinpoint the location of these 'London Scottish' volunteers. The tents in the middle distance are pitched on what today is the northern end of St Andrews Road.

Ten
Durrington and Salvington

Durrington Lane, looking south towards the Lamb inn. Durrington was not as important as Broadwater or Tarring, but, until the 1790s, it was larger than Worthing, and, unlike Worthing, was a parish in its own right. During the thirteenth century, Durrington developed as a centre for the cider industry: the parish was dominated by orchards. The increasing popularity of beer during Tudor times, however, brought about a marked decline in cider drinking in Sussex. Durrington was not incorporated into the Borough of Worthing until 1929. It is from this date that its rural identity was rapidly eroded.

The Old Smithy at Durrington. This building still survives, standing on the northern side of Salvington Road from the Lamb.

The pond at Half Moon Lane, Salvington - not Durrington as stated on this postcard. During the course of the present century, as the urban centre has expanded, Worthing has lost all its old ponds, but, thanks to the efforts of Mrs Wallace of Salvington, the Northbrook Pond at West Durrington was saved from being filled in 1988.

A view of Durrington's pond. Notice the thatched cottage in the background.

The ruins of Durrington Chapel. During the religious and political turmoil following the English Civil Wars of the 1640s, many congregations found themselves out of sympathy with the views and beliefs of their priests. Such was the case at Durrington, where the incumbent was expelled. There then followed a protracted dispute between the parish and the authorities. Eventually the chapel was abandoned and allowed to fall into ruination, the parishioners being advised to attend divine service at Tarring instead.

Can this really be Durrington? A hazy savannah, today transformed into one of the largest concentrations of residential housing in Sussex.

The junction of Arundel Road (A27) with Durrington Hill in the 1920s. The road had recently been metalled, but where are the cars?

Swandean Hospital. Originally built as an Isolation Hospital, following the Worthing typhoid epidemic of 1893, a hundred years ago this was a lonely spot; staff from the hospital, cycling down into Worthing, were issued with stout cudgels to protect themselves on the lonely journey down wooded lanes to the town.

Lacies Cottage, scandalously demolished in 1956, following a small fire. Not only one of the oldest buildings in the Borough, but also associated with one of the area's most famous inhabitants - John Selden. Selden was born in the cottage in 1584 and in later life exercised a great influence on the theological and philosophical ideas of his times. An inscription above the doorway, written in Latin by Selden, welcomed the honest visitor, but rebuked any arriving with thieving intent.

A vigilant observer might be able to identify the house in the picture, now certainly surrounded by other similar properties in High Salvington. The author would certainly be pleased to hear from anyone who can place this view.

Worthing's last surviving windmill. By the 1920s windmills were becoming so scarce that a movement was afoot to preserve them.

Inside Salvington Mill in about 1930, by that time converted into Tea Rooms. Today the mill is owned by a trust, which has restored it to its original condition. There are regular open-days and flour is still occasionally ground.

Salvington Hill between the wars. A lonely figure pushes a heavy load homewards.

105

Salvington Road in the late 1930s, just before road widening transformed the scene.

'Medical Mission' to High Salvington sounds like the work of missionaries in darkest Africa, rather than the northern part of Worthing. Yet before the First World War ignorance was a major cause of disease. Some people still clung to superstitious remedies and few could afford the fees of a General Practitioner.

Edwardian ladies wander at ease over the Downs north of Worthing, with not a house or car in sight.

A view across the Findon Valley to Cissbury Ring in the early 1920s.

FROM BOST HILL, HIGH SALVINGTON, WORTHING.

By the late 1920s, development was beginning to creep along the valley and over Bost Hill.

The middle classes, seeking a commuter base in the country, or a retirement home near the sea, came in their thousands to settle in the new housing estates built around Worthing between the wars.

Eleven
Goring

Goring was separated more from Worthing than either Broadwater, Tarring, or even Durrington, by simple virtue of the fact that over a mile of countryside lay between Goring and the houses in Mill Road. Paul Schweder, the owner of Courtlands, was so hostile to Worthing that he went to extraordinary lengths in the years before the Great War to frustrate efforts by the Worthing Gas Company to run a main to Goring. The date and place of this photograph, as well as the nature of the work taking place, suggests that it could be connected with the famous dispute, which was eventually only settled as a result of court action. Goring church can be seen in the right-hand corner.

Goring Lane
(Autumn)

Goring Lane (now Road) in about 1910. To try and confound the Gas Company, Schweder had a tunnel dug under Goring Lane, forcing the Company to lay the main nearer the surface. Schweder then employed a steam traction engine to pass backwards and forwards over the surface, until the main was crushed. His enemies got their revenge during the war, when he was charged, though later acquitted, of spying for the Germans. Some local people had claimed he was seen signalling from Courtlands to German submarines in the Channel.

After Schweder's death, his estate was sold and later developed for housing. Many of the roads in this part of Goring are named after Schweder's children, grandchildren, nieces, and nephews, examples being: Patricia, Alinora, Harvey, Angus, Gerald and Aglaia. The attractive little lodge stood to the north of Courtlands, set just back from Goring Lane. It was demolished as recently as 1963.

Children fishing in Goring Brook at the turn of the century. The Court House and Goring Church can be seen in the background.

An early view of Sea Lane. Until the early 1930s, when the Goring Hall Estate was sold, a high wall ran down Sea Lane, behind which trees were planted along its length. Today those same trees form the central reservation of the dual carriageway.

Another view of Sea Lane, looking northwards. In the distance the Court House can be seen to the left and Peacock Hall to the right. Peacock Hall was demolished in the late 1930s, as were the cottages. The Mulberry Hotel now stands on the site.

COFFINS LEAVING, GORING CHURCH.

This faded photograph recalls the tragic death of three young village labourers, killed by lightning in 1907, while sheltering under a tree close to Highdown. Here we see the funeral cortège leaving Goring Church.

Goring Street looking northwards from the Bull Inn. Nothing seen in this photograph survives today. Following the sale of the estate, the wholesale destruction of the old village took place. The process was interrupted by the War and re-commenced afterwards.

Markwick's Stores stood on the western side of Goring Street, close to the junction with Jupp's Lane (now Goring Way). The shop stocked everything from boots to packets of sweets.

113

Villagers pose outside cottages close to the present-day Aldsworth roundabout. All but one of the cottages and buildings in this part of Goring have been demolished. The old Forge went as recently as 1966.

Three Goring worthies of 1907. Born and bred in the village, all were in their eighties when this photograph was taken. The oldest, Mus Martin, appears to be the most nimble, as he is standing, while his two friends, one with two sticks placed in front of him, remain seated.

Goring railway station in a very rural setting. Even the signal box has yet to be built. The railway came to Goring in 1846 and cut the parish in half, isolating Northbrook and Limbrick from the rest of the village. Crossings were however provided by the new station and at Limbrick Lane.

Goring signal box was built in 1906. Following the listing of a signal box at Plumpton, British Rail, fearful of having any more of its railway buildings protected for posterity, acted swiftly. During the course of one night in 1988, the signal boxes at Goring, West Worthing and Worthing were demolished.

Goring Cross Ways, looking north up Titnore Lane. To the left is the Littlehampton Road, which today is the busy A259 dual carriageway. The cottage to the right is the old toll house.

Goring Cross Roads. 84.

Cross Ways looking south. The track marks of passing vehicles can be seen in the dirt of this unmade road. The lady in the photograph would not recognise this view today. Apart from the thundering A259, she would also be amazed by the hundreds of flats, houses and a college campus that now spread over what were then fields.

116

Goring beach in about 1929. In this year Goring Parish Council agreed to be incorporated into the Borough of Worthing. The increasing number of people living on the seashore in old railway carriages, caravans and tents, exasperated the parish council. Worthing promised to end ad-hoc development and to preserve Goring's character. Never were more false words said in earnest.

The cafe on Goring Beach, at the end of Sea Lane, was a popular rendezvous. The present-day cafe was built in 1966, amidst loud protests from residents, who objected to such a permanent structure blocking the sea view. Goring councillors at this time actually won and lost elections on the issue.

Sea Place looking northwards in about 1930. The present-day Eirene Road is to the right, where the boys are standing. The present-day road to the left, Marine Drive, had not been built at this time.

Sea Place, looking towards the sea. Sea Place Stores, which is now a tea room, is to the left. The flint wall marks the ancient boundary between the Manor of Sea Place and that of Goring.

Twelve
Children

Life for children and young adults has changed more dramatically than for the rest of the population. Infant mortality was rife in the last century, when the death of a son or daughter was the norm, rather than the exception. Education, once the prerogative of parents and the Church, became a matter for the State in 1870, with the first of the Education Acts, which culminated in the 1901 Act, increasing the school leaving age to fourteen. For young adults, referred to as 'the rising generation' in Victorian times and as teenagers since the 1950s, the days of deference and apprenticeship are long since over. The crowded school scene in this photograph of about 1900 was taken in Worthing, but the actual school is not known.

A class of six pupils. Not a State school, of course, but Charmandean, a private school for girls north of Broadwater. Notice the picture of George V on the wall, between the two windows.

Charmandean pupils, engaging in artistic dancing on the school lawns. Charmandean was one of Worthing's great houses. After the school closed, the land was sold off for development and eventually Charmandean House, like Offington Hall, was demolished.

In the last century and the early years of this century, Bonfire Night and Carnival were two great days for poorer children. The woman on the right appears somewhat pensive, no doubt hoping the children will keep still while the photograph is taken.

Children in a fancy-dress competition at Broadwater in 1908. Contestant 101 looks thoroughly fed up.

More mummers, at the same fete, this time some heavily disguised adult revellers.

Children on the seafront, by the Royal Sea House Hotel, which means this photograph must pre-date the fire of 1901. The flags indicate a celebration, possibly Queen Victoria's Jubilee of 1897.

A mother and her children on the beach near Splash Point in about 1905. Note the confident pose and expression of the boy. Clearly a well-to-do family.

On the sands at low tide. Messing around in the rock pools is a pleasure children still enjoy, although the number of fishing boats on the seashore is now greatly reduced.

Three children sitting on the capstan arm about a hundred years ago. Despite its grainy quality, the photograph seems to capture something of the playfulness of the children. Notice the small child standing by the capstan: although dressed like a girl he is probably a little boy - such was the fashion for very young children at that time.

The official opening of Worthing Hospital's purpose-built Children's Ward by Mrs Lloyd, the wife of a prominent local landowner and JP. She is seated on the right-hand side of the table.

The Children's Ward was regarded as state of the art in the 1930s. In 1906 infant mortality in Worthing stood at 109 per thousand births; by 1936 it had fallen to 33.

Children in Orme Road in about 1907, in the times when it was safe to play in the street.

Today this would be thought not politically correct! Children blacked up for Carnival outside the Old Palace at Tarring. Even the little 'bride' has a blackened face. By Edwardian times the more threatening and anarchic side of mummery had been tempered and controlled, but a hint of the old ways still remained.

Children outside the Reading Room at Goring, opposite the Bull Inn. The girl in the centre is Daisy Waite, whom Terry Child found to be still alive in 1989, aged 96. She had sent this view as a birthday card to her grandmother in 1907.

Daisy Waite, sitting at the end of the second row on the left-hand side of this postcard. Daisy also sent this card to her grandmother, this time at Christmas. On the back she asked her grandma to try and find her face in the picture. She also said that she would be hanging up her stocking that night. Tellingly, she added, 'We have got a fortnight holiday from school and I do not want to go back'. Evidently the Master and the Governess were not to her liking.

The Boys Brigade, like the Boy Scouts, were an attempt by the Edwardians to instil in youth a sense of religious purpose and military duty. This tight control over young minds was something of an aberration, however. The 'youth rebellion' of the 1950s was only an echo of earlier times, when Bonfire Boys ran amock, and 'rough music' was a frequent occurrence.

Football has remained a youthful passion since its emergence in a modern form in the 1880s. Although the presence of two clergymen in a modern-day youth team photograph is perhaps less likely.

The Sussex Pig.

You may push me
You may shuv
But I'm hanged
If I'll be druv
From WORTHING.

Never end a local history book on too serious a note. This humorous postcard from earlier this century not only reminds us that our sacred animal is the pig and that Sussex people 'wunt be druv', but also that real Worthing people will always be 'Pork Bolters'.